D0905343

# Rumplesnakeskin

written by Charlotte Guillain ☆ illustrated by Dawn Beacon

Raintree

Chicago, Illinois

© 2014 Raintree
an imprint of Capstone Global Library, LLC
Chicago, Illinois

To contact Capstone Global Library please call 800-747-4992, or visit our web site
www.capstonepub.com

All rights reserved. No part of this publication may be reproduced or transmitted in any
form or by any means, electronic or mechanical, including photocopying, recording,
taping, or any information storage and retrieval system, without permission in writing from
the publisher.

Edited by Daniel Nunn, Rebecca Rissman, and Catherine Veitch
Designed by Joanna Hinton-Malivoire
Original illustrations © Capstone Global Library, Ltd, 2014
Illustrated by Dawn Beacon
Production by Victoria Fitzgerald
Originated by Capstone Global Library, Ltd
Printed and bound in China

17 16 15 14 13
10 9 8 7 6 5 4 3 2 1

**Library of Congress Cataloging-in-Publication Data**
Guillain, Charlotte.
  Rumplesnakeskin / Charlotte Guillain.
     pages cm.—(Animal fairy tales)
ISBN 978-1-4109-6111-2 (hb)—ISBN 978-1-4109-6118-1 (pb) [1. Fairy tales. 2. Folklore—
Germany.] I. Rumpelstiltskin (Folk tale) English. II. Title.
PZ8.G947Rum 2014
398.2—dc23                    2013011751
[E]

Every effort has been made to contact copyright holders of material reproduced in
this book. Any omissions will be rectified in subsequent printings if notice is given to
the publisher.

# Characters

Sybil

Sybil's Father

King

Rumplesnakeskin

Prince

Once upon a time, there lived a
beautiful squirrel named Sybil.
Her father liked to boast about Sybil,
telling everyone how wonderful she
was. One day he even said that Sybil
could turn acorns into gold!

Of course, it wasn't true! But when the king heard the story, he called Sybil to the palace and shut her in a room full of acorns.

"Turn the acorns into gold by morning or I will chop off your beautiful bushy tail," he ordered.

The king's son, a handsome prince, begged his father not to hurt Sybil.

Sybil sat on the floor and cried.
All of a sudden, a snake appeared
before her.

"Lissssten! I will turn the acornsssss
into gold if you give me your
necklace," he hissed. Sybil agreed.

In the morning, the room was full of golden acorns, and the king was very happy. But then he took Sybil to a bigger room, with an even bigger pile of acorns inside.

"Turn the acorns into gold by morning or I will chop off your beautiful bushy tail," the king demanded.

Again, Sybil sat on the floor and cried. But all of a sudden, the snake appeared again.

"Missssssss! I will turn the acornsssss into gold if you give me your ring," he hissed. Sybil agreed.

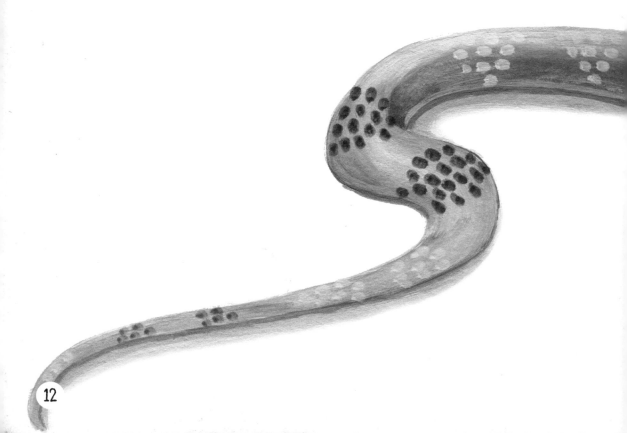

In the morning, the room was full of golden acorns again. The king was delighted. He took Sybil to an enormous room filled with yet more acorns.

This time he said, "If you turn these acorns into gold by morning you may marry my son, the prince. But if you fail, I will chop off your beautiful bushy tail."

Once more, Sybil sat on the floor and cried. Once more, the snake slithered into the room. But this time, Sybil had nothing left to give him.

"I will turn the acornsssss into gold if
you promisssse to give me your first baby
sssssquirrel," said the snake slyly. Sybil
sadly agreed.

In the morning, the room was full of golden acorns. Sybil and the prince were married. But when a baby was born, the snake returned.

Sybil begged him not to take her baby. "You have three chancessss to guesssss my name," hissed the snake. "If you guessss correctly, you can keep your baby."

On the following two mornings, Sybil tried to guess the snake's name, but she was wrong both times.

On the third morning, Sybil heard the snake singing outside.
He sang, "She'll never win this guesssssing game, Rumplesssssnakeskin is my name!"

RUMPLESNAKESKIN

Sybil hid her excitement as the snake slithered in.

"One more guessss," he hissed.

"Um...is your name...Rumplesnakeskin?" asked Sybil.

The snake gave a hiss of rage! He was so angry that his skin split in two and he hurried away, leaving just his snakeskin behind. And Sybil, the prince, and their baby lived happily ever after.

**The End**

# Where does this story come from?

You've probably already heard the story that *Rumplesnakeskin* is based on—*Rumplestiltskin*. There are many different versions of this story. When people tell a story, they often make little changes to make it their own. How would you change this story?

## The history of the story

*Rumplestiltskin* was first written down by the Brothers Grimm. Jacob (1785–1863) and Wilhelm (1786–1859) Grimm lived near the city of Frankfurt, in Germany. They collected and wrote down many fairy stories and folktales. These tales were told by storytellers who entertained people in the days before radio and television.

In the original story, a miller boasts to the king about his daughter, claiming that she can spin straw into gold. The king shuts the daughter away in a tower filled with straw and a spinning wheel. He tells her to spin the straw into gold by morning or he will chop off her head. The girl despairs, but then a strange creature appears and offers to spin the straw into gold in return for the girl's necklace. In the morning, the king takes the girl to an even bigger room, full of more straw. The creature appears again and helps the girl in return for her ring. On the third day, the girl is shut in an even bigger room full of straw, but this time she has nothing to give the creature in return for his help. In the end, she promises her firstborn child to him if he will spin the straw into gold again. In the morning, the girl is released. She marries the king and becomes queen. But when she has a child, the creature reappears and demands that she keep her promise. When she begs for mercy, he gives her three chances to guess his name—if she guesses correctly she can keep her baby. He comes back the next two mornings, but the queen cannot guess his name. On the final night, the queen's messenger is riding through the forest when he hears the creature singing a song that includes his name. The messenger passes this on to the queen, who is able to tell the creature what his name is on the third morning. Rumplestiltskin leaves empty-handed in a rage, and the queen lives happily ever after.